This book belongs to:

____

84371595R00068

Made in the USA
San Bernardino, CA
07 August 2018